WHERE WE GOING?

A collection of poems inspired by Marvin Gaye's album, "What's Going On"

TIMOTHY D. JONES

©2021 Timothy D. Jones

All rights reserved. No potion of this book may be reproduced, stored in a retrieval system, or transmitted in any form or by any means, including photocopying, recording, or other electronic or mechanical methods, except for brief quotations in critical reviews or articles, without prior written permission of the author.

What's Going On by Marvin Gaye. Released May 21, 1971 by Tamla. All rights reserved.

All scriptures are from the New King James Version ®. Copyright © 1982 by Thomas Nelson. Used by permission. All rights reserved.

TITLE	PAGE
Introduction	4
What's Going On	14
What's Happening Brother	24
Flyin' High (In The Friendly Skies)	29
Save The Children	36
God is Love	44
Mercy Mercy Me (The Ecology)	51
Right On	56
Wholy Holy	64
Inner City Blues (Make Me Wanna Holler)	71
Where Are We Going	78

Introduction

This project has been in my spirit and my heart for a number of years. I have gone through so many iterations of creative ways to showcase my admiration for Marvin Gaye's *"What's Going On"* album. In the midst of my contemplation that at times became procrastination, I would find myself in a state of frustration. Part of my frustration was dealing with the self-doubt challenging my worthiness to even do a project that would be presented as a direct tribute to one of the greatest albums ever made. Over the years I would mention the thought of creating a work as an ode to *"What's Going On"* to people that I am close to and they would always offer a word of support. The struggle to make this come to life was a battle within myself that I was determined to win. I decided that there was no way that I would allow the 50th anniversary of *"What's Going On?"* come without me offering my contribution to the world.

A few months ago, I shared my idea for this project to a close friend of mine, Blink who I had done some groundbreaking creative projects with back in the late 1990s. It's interesting that when you fully commit to forging ahead that oftentimes the fuel to push you forward comes from looking back. My friend became my creative partner in the project. If nothing else, this would help keep me accountable to deadlines so that the project would be done on time to be released on May 21, 2021 to commemorate the 50th anniversary of the release *"What's Going On"*.

My book would be entitled "Where are we going?" which is a title of one of the songs on the "You're the Man" album that was recorded by Marvin Gaye as a socially conscious follow up to the *"What's Going On"* album. The follow up album was recorded in 1972 but was not officially released until 2019. It was released in celebration of what would've been Marvin's 80th birthday. I was inspired by the song 'Where are we going?" and I didn't want to title my work, *"What's Going On?"*. When I listened to "Where are we going?" I kept thinking of Dr. King's book, "Where do we go from here?" I believed that this work could be a continuation of a critical conversation that would arise when pondering the question of "where are we going?" of " where do we go from here?" Now I had decided on the title of the book, but I hadn't committed to what type of book it would become.

In reading the insert to the double CD 30th anniversary version of *'What's Going On"* Smokey Robinson recalls Marvin telling him that he left the door open, and that God was writing this album. The image of Marvin in the studio creating with the door cracked open so that God could come back and forth unannounced has stayed with me for years. I wanted to have the same experience in working on my project. To some this may seem like a tall order but for others who engage in the creative process and understand that creativity is a very spiritual experience; it isn't as far-fetched as it may sound. Every spirit that is present when one is creating is not of God, but I am able to discern the difference and be led accordingly.

As I started to write I was engaged in the process of deciding on which voice of mine I should use, and this would influence the style of writing. In my work I often interact with individuals who are scholars and members of the academy. Do I work on developing my academic voice and speak in the form of essays infused with research, critical analysis and the posing of thought? I am an ordained minister and in my listening to *"What's Going On"* I always hear the Holy Spirit speaking to me and bringing scriptures to my mind. So, do I write a series of sermons that intertwine my takeaways from the lyrics of the songs with scriptures in an attempt to minister in writing to those who may not sit in a pew or log on to hear a sermon? I am an MC and a lifelong lover of Hip-Hop and I am known for my ability to freestyle. I call myself an 'In the moment" MC. Do I write songs based on my interpretation of the songs and make an album to honor this great album?

I began the writing process by writing in an essay format and then reviewing songs and writing down scripture references. As I was writing I was having weekly conversations with my creative partner and I was finding myself not fully committed to the writing style that I was engaging in during the early stages of this book. My conversations with Blink were key because while I was trying to figure out my voice and method of writing, he was figuring out how to create music that would accompany the audio version of this book. We were clear on what we didn't want to do which is a start. This start wasn't getting us closer to what we wanted to do so we kept talking, believing that our breakthrough would come to pass.

Then it happened; Blink and I were talking, and I began to talk about what *"What's Going On"* means to me and why. I went back to my start back in 1996 as a member of Writers Corps (shout out to Kenny Carroll) where I was tasked with teaching creative writing workshops at Options Public Charter School in Washington DC. I had never taught before and I could count my creative writing experience on one hand with fingers to spare. What I did know was Hip-Hop and I had a growing interest in Soul music. I had heard the song *"What's Going On"* in the past but I hadn't spent time with it in a way where it was speaking to my soul and influencing how I saw myself and the world around me. This sentiment was about to drastically change, and I would never be the same moving forward.

I created a curriculum that I called "Beat 2 the Rhyme" (B2TR). B2TR is a curriculum where I select songs based on themes and then invite the students to complete various creative writing activities as ways to express themselves based on the selected themes. As I learned about various figurative language devices, I would implement them into my activities. As I was building the curriculum while teaching it, I would visit the record store weekly and look for new music and talk to the owner of the store. In my own way I began to dig through CDs the way I would stand in amazement as producers would explain their crate digging process to find the right sound that would spark their next hit.

The greatest find that was realized was the *"What's Going On"* album. When I learned more about Marvin Gaye's roots growing up in Washington DC, I knew I had to introduce this work to my students. In addition to teaching at Options Public Charter School, I began my career in Youth work at Martha's Table. Martha's

Table was a non-profit community based organization located on 14th Street NW in Washington DC. The location was significant because it was around the corner and down the street from the high school that Marvin Gaye attended. I now had this great album in my hands and was working in the neighborhood where Marvin attended high school.

In 1996, the album was 25 years old. I decided that I would present selected songs from the album to my students without telling them that the songs they were listening to were 25 years old. In my class we would read the lyrics to the song without the music first and then we would listen to the music while following along with the words. The words to the songs in *"What's Going On"* were so relevant to the communities and the lives of my students, they thought I was sharing a new release. My students were amazed when I revealed to them that the songs they were listening to, discussing and writing to were 25 years old. These 5th and 6th graders hadn't experienced music as something that was timeless. Music was snapshots of the moment lasting for as long as they were deemed popular.

To connect with my students and to help develop my confidence in my abilities to teach creative writing, I began to write poems as examples to include in my lessons. I wrote under the pseudonym "OpTIMuS." (I chose Optimus because I Transformers was my favorite cartoon), I was transforming myself from an accountant to an educator and my name is Timothy. I explained "OpTIMuS" as it's the opportunity and time for us and whatever was going to happen in my class, Tim was going to be in the middle. The pseudonym provided a level of protection because if the students didn't like the work, I would stop including it without anyone knowing it was me.

At the end of the school year, I let the students know that OpTIMuS and I were one in the same. Some of the students speculated that it was me all along because as they learned about writing in voice, they said the writings sounded like me. It was a high point in my early teaching and youth development career that I still hold near to my heart. The students encouraged me to continue with B2TR and to keep writing as OpTIMuS.

This is why "Where are we going?" is a collection of poems. I spent so much time trying to decide which voice to speak in and to whom I am speaking to and in the end I was led back to where I began. What better way to pay homage to the album that has helped guide me through live decisions for the past 25 years than speaking in the voice that I used when we first met. It is my prayer that you will be moved by reading and or listening to the collection of 10 poems that have been written to take us back to bring us forward.

Marvin, thank you for your obedience to God in the moments that your partnership was creating an album that would serve as an atlas for our community and society at large. Over the past 50 years your words and melodies have provided us warnings and wisdom. The relevance of the warnings in the wisdom in many ways hasn't been heeded but God is forever faithful which allows us to still press towards the mark of the prize of the high calling in Jesus Christ. Like you said, "don't talk about my father, God is my friend."

Thank you, Brother Marvin, for loving us enough to speak from your heart and making a timeless piece of art. The breath of your inspiration was never contained in your physical frame so forever years from now, your words will continue to remain.

What's Going On

The inquiry of an "in your face" mystery

Has been asked in song for half a century

Is the question based on an observation upon arrival

Or a question in hopes of figuring out a plan for survival

Is the question an ignition for change

Or an attempt to see if what you're seeing seems strange

Frustration and pain attempting to rob me of faith and hope

Suffering is the ink in the pen as I write

Could it be that the question is the light

The dawning of a new day after a seemingly endless night

Do I see more of the wreckage left behind or the promises that lie ahead

Are the promises the results of change or the guarantee of things remaining the same

Tired of being beaten for wanting a life consisting of more than breathing

Looking for an equal shot at achieving instead of an unequal shot at being shot

It has been said that you put out fire with water and only love can conquer hate

Others have said, there's a war going on and nobody's safe

Racial advancements at times feels like running in place

Training for a race with a map of a course that is out of date

When I feel overwhelmed and need clarity

I go and spend some time with Marvin

I hum along to what's going on?

I hold them as the making of my anthem that keeps me pressing on

I take in the words as more than lyrics to a song

I talk to him to let him know that many of the headlines of what was wrong are still going on

I listen with the song on repeat expecting to hear something different every time that Marvin speaks

On one time I heard the party in the introduction, and I closed my eyes to imagine it was a Friday or Saturday night

The slapping of hands in unison with the chant of "What's Happening?"

Survived a long week of work or frustration of pounding the pavement in search of an occupation

Watching the news to see if what happened on your street was deemed worthy of mentioning to the community at large

Having to be your own reporter to let your friends know what's going on

Turn the music up because downstairs those brothers and sisters are talking about revolution again

I just want to leave trouble behind and enjoy the night with friends

Hey, how are you doing? I haven't seen you before. What's your name?

By the look on your face, you can't hear what I'm saying over the music that is playing

Maybe I will use the groove as my choreographer of my next move

As I approach, I froze as Marvin hit that note that everybody quotes

Talking about mothers crying because of brothers dying

Is this a party or a meeting because if it's the later then I'm leaving

Bringing us together to talk about a crazy world outside is a drink I don't want to consume

I just want to party and have a good time with everyone in this room

Next thing I know I'm sitting in chair nodding my head with my eyes closed

I thought I was coming to get funky but now I'm getting food for my soul

In a room with some cats from the other side of tracks listening to Marvin break down where we're at

Mothers, Brothers, Fathers and Sisters. Police, Protestors, Parishioners and Politicians

Let's take a moment to LISTEN

We are living in a moment where what is love is constantly under attack

And the cracks of the whips have become the thuds of sticks on the backs of blacks

Brave soldiers coming home finding the hood is in worse shape than where they were just at

Protest to protect,

protest to correct,

protest to connect,

protest for respect,

protest for what's next...

Living in a world where nothing seems to be going right

So many enemies it's hard to decide which way to fight

Being told that we're wrong before we even speak a word

Being told that we're wrong because we're young and have too much nerve

So many songs talking about war being wrong

When it's weapons and retaliation we need to stand up to stop it

When it's wisdom and respect we need to stand up to protect it

When it's wealth and reallocation we need to stand up to create it

When it's working and realization we need to stand up to save it

Love is a power and love is a force

Love is a navigator that charts its own course

Love has been battered, scarred and bruised but never defeated

Love is passed on like a priceless family treasure

Love is what keeps us going on and staying in the fight together

Love gives a vision of how we can be living if we practice sacrifice and giving

Hate distorts your view of life to the point where you find peace in killing

Nothing is more tragic that the habit of aiming guns at mirrors

Susceptible to the snare that lies telling us that no one will care if we're gone

I have to thank Marvin for making our vision clearer

So we can clearly see what's going on?

And now that I have your full attention, can I play another song?

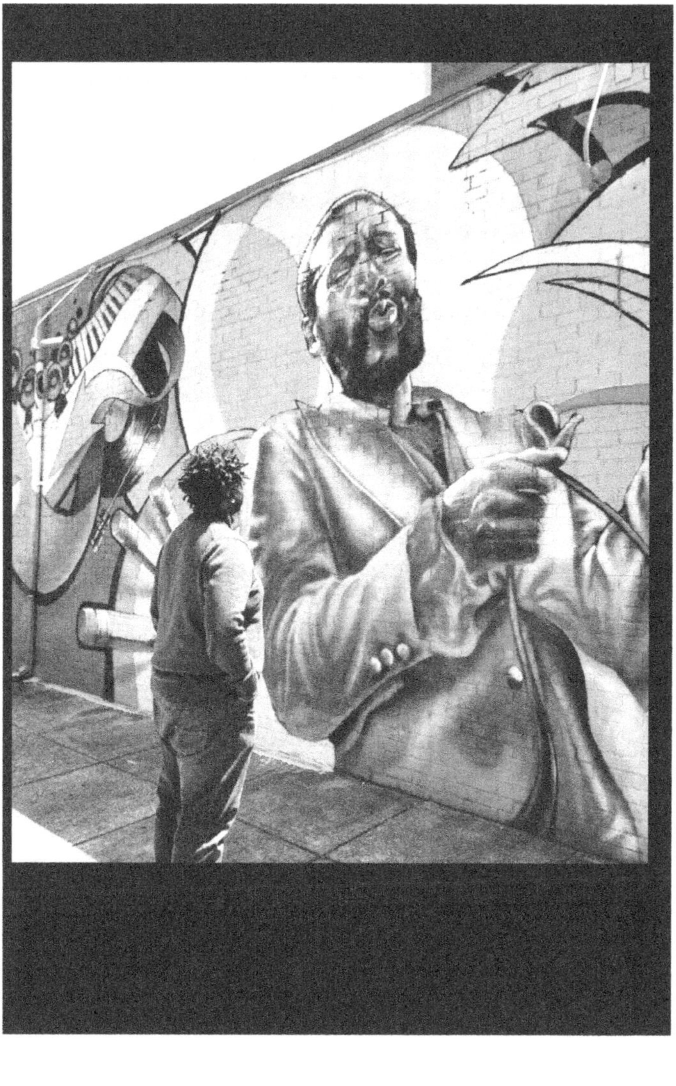

WHAT'S HAPPENING BROTHER

A song that was written as a discussion led by a brother coming home from war
Questions posed from what's happening on the political, neighborhood and even sports scenes
Based on what I'm seeing am I awake or living in a dream

Visions of memories of how we used to get down and dance and live life by chance
Hanging on the corners chasing romance hearing the sounds of sirens and the ambulance

Chalk lines for hopscotch and the finish lines of someone's life
Picket lines for protesting and for striking against poor treatment on the job
Are those brothers on the corner still plotting on how to rob

I apologize for going on with my questions without checking on your direction
What's Happening with you my friend, how in the world have you been?

It's great to see a familiar face in a place that doesn't quite look the same
I feel the change, but I don't know if it's a change for the better
I hear people screaming "Black Power" but is it keeping us together?

The complications that exist for generations provide different paths to a similar destination

For a while certain words weren't said to my face but life is still a race about race

Now it's a fight to decide on which fight is right and how to treat those who left
I remember when the motivation was to simply figure out how to get out
Based on the lessons learned we were told to never return but never forget

Well which one is it? Keep the block in my heart while abandoning my part?
I went away to school and it's been so long
Took a trip back and now even the feeling is gone

Claiming a sense of ownership on something that's hard to recognize
Ra said "It ain't where you're from, it's where you're at"
If that's the case, then what do I do with this desire to return back
Reminisce on remains while observing surroundings that seem strange

TELL ME what's happening before it makes the headlines

TELL ME what's happening that has nothing to do with hate or crime

TELL ME what's happening that will make me appreciate time

TELL ME what's happening based on God's design

TELL ME what's happening so I can understand where we're going

TELL ME what's happening so I can know what they're not showing

TELL ME what's happening so I can feel the love again

TELL ME what's happening so I know you're still my friend

The truth is what was once happening may never happen again
The neighborhood done got split wide open over this happening again

"This" can be the violence, the silence,
the neglect and or the disrespect
Maybe what's happening is a reality
check

Where the dots connect to a reflection
and perception of what is and will remain
real
If we don't find a way to feel and heal
from the pain
What's happening (repeat and fade)

Flyin' High
(In The Friendly Sky)

Good afternoon, this is your pilot speaking
Let me be the first to welcome you to flight
zero/zero/zero/zero
We are finishing our safety check and once we
have the all clear
We will be taking off out of here

As we begin our ascension upward, we ask that you remain seated
There is no need to look out of the windows
Because it's what's outside your window that led you to this flight
If you can just close your eyes everything will seem right
Let me warn you… don't close your eyes to look at yourself on the inside
Some say that if you look at yourself with your eyes closed you can see your soul

Our destination for today's flight may require us to stop to refuel
You know that each time we lift off it takes a little more fuel to reach our desired altitude
No matter how far we go our destination will be the same as our origination
All checked bags will be returned and some items may shift during the flight
Items may be lost or stolen and you may find new items in your mental overhead bin

The turbulence that you may feel is very real
even if it is in your imagination
Traveling to change your situation versus
your location will always lead to frustration
Beginning the flight thinking you're a master
to realize that you're a slave
At least you will be able to feel that pain before
you end up in a grave
A dead slave is slavery twice because you lost
your soul and your life
Your time in the sky will feel so friendly but
when you land you will feel empty

Wait, haven't I seen you before, weren't you
just here?
What are you looking for that you can't seem
to find?
There is no place in my flight's GPS called
"Peace of mind."
Man, I have enough conscious that I don't
even want your money
This is a flight that I know that you can't afford

It maybe time for you to untangle this umbilical cord
There isn't any life for you here believe me when I say
Look around and ask the other passengers what is today?

Voluntary submission is the beginning of addiction
Addiction distorts reality's position within our cognition
Craving something to take me away that leaves me deeper right where I stand
Holding death in my hands thinking that my life is still under my command
The feeling of being forsaken by the choices that I'm making
The substances that I'm taking and the promises that I'm breaking
Can I muster the strength to look at myself in the mirror
To see myself a little clearer

Deal with the vision of my vision based on how I'm living
I punch the glass to see a jagged reflection which a clearer representation
Of my life at the moment
There I said it, I'm gonna own it
What do I do when this flight touches down
And I've never left the ground
I almost laid my body down but then I heard in the distance a sound
This needle dropped on the record of past prayers that I prayed
Filled with promises that I made standing over my mother's grave
I need to find the path that her prayers paved
Find the Lord that she told me about that saves

Which way do you turn when the lessons of life have finally been learned?
Will the morning be alright if I make it through the night

Or will the morning just be the misery within me in plain sight

Who is willing to help someone who doesn't trust themselves?

Who is willing to see past my self inflicted scars to see an injured soul?

Who is willing to see me as human regardless of what I was consuming?

Who is willing to direct me back to God whose love for me never changed?

No more flying high to get by
because this flight is a lie
No more friendly skies no more living lies
(repeat and fade out)

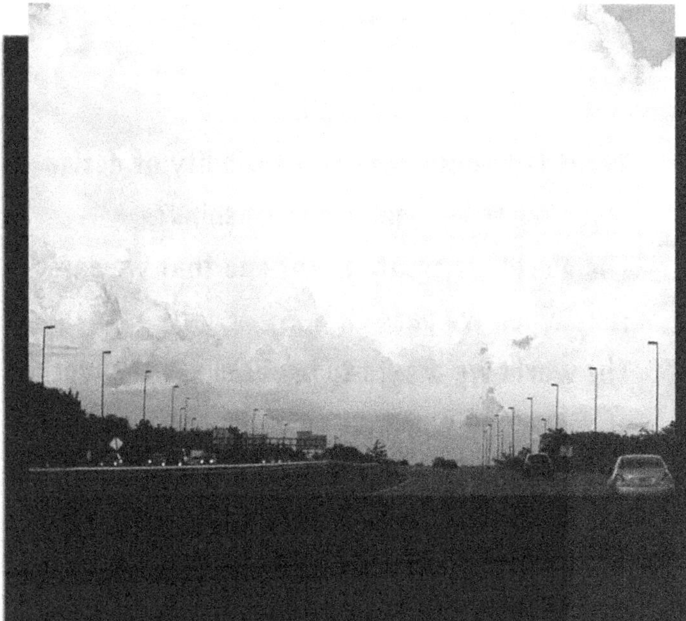

Save The Children

What is the inherent responsibility of design when what you make is left behind?
The world we create is not one that we can take when we pass on
The world we create today becomes the world of tomorrow when we're gone
The notion of having to save the children is one that is an indictment of our choices
Children having a need to be saved before they even have voices
Is saving children a call for us to stop doing/more than a call to start doing?
What would a world be if we prioritize the ones with the most innocence in their eyes?
How painful is the light of truth when we've been living through visions of lies?

I believe the children have the capacity to save
us more than us saving them
I've seen what the birth of child can do to men
For the women that nurture our children to go
further in the midst of murder
Saving the children is a large part of their
reason for breathing
We create the horrible conditions then condemn
the choices made by children for living
Where the solution of sentences over
opportunities and supports are given
We marvel at the beauty that the children have
created in the absence of us being there
Then we arrive in disguise dangling lies as the
prize offering only one when thousands will try
Only the strong will survive while skewing
what is strength and survival
You better not live in this world with heart
even though its beat is vital

Where is the soul of a nation built on the backs
of people determined not to be equal?

And each generation writes the script and
shoots the next sequel
Flowers represent life but are given to bring joy to
the receiver by separating them from their roots
The joy is short lived as the elements bring
forth the flower's imminent death
Is this the plight for our children once they take
their first breath?
Or do we create a world where there is plenty
of fertile ground
And wherever the child looks there is love to be
found
Most importantly, we create a world where a
child will see love when they look in the mirror
A reflection of God's perfection and not an
image that to world deems them inferior

To live for the children is a pattern that first
requires a healing so that we don't resent
What the world did to us when we were
children

I had it rough and look what it did for me/ Pull yourself up and make your own way
Big said it best in "things done changed" when in the hood the parents look at the children strange
We've destroyed the connection to their souls so now we fight to establish control
Creating a world full of holes while trying to feel whole
The cycles of hate and despair always seem to be there when you say that you care
It's amazing that the children somehow have the resiliency to bear the load
That's placed upon them most often to no fault of their own
Left alone to turn a house into a home or a seat to throne
Propaganda's prey of a domestic war targeting the royalty within their DNA
I'm on a quest to resurrect potential from the graveyards of the mental
Profound words being spoken on top of instrumentals

So children can see themselves as instruments
playing the scales of confidence
That harmonize with the evidence that they are
heaven sent

If we truly see our children as gems and jewels
then we'd be more conscious of our schools
A drop off and a pick-up with very little focus
on what happens in between
Standardized by standards that lie measuring
achievement on one's ability to comply
Stripping the beauty of the garden whose
standards were a sea of radiant colors
The fact that different seeds can be planted
into the same earth given the same water
And bloom to what it is destined to be is the
definition of free that our children need
To the one who plants there is a divine reason
for the rain
To the one that overcomes there is a divine
reason for the pain

I've realized that if we live for the children
then we will never die
The existence of our persistence will ultimately
multiply
The world is passing away, but we decide if the
world possess our hope
What I see doesn't define, blind, bind or confine me
I close my eyes at times so that my vision can
be clearer
Spend a little time looking inside at God's soul mirror
An inspection of imperfection that comes with
directions
Now I can see that saving the children is really
preserving me
Not with the expectation of something in return
Just the process of adding roots to the flowers
of lessons learned
What was my dead end road now has an HOV
and a turn

We must see the pain past the armor
Recognize the truth in karma

That today is a segway into tomarra'
And that love and hope are worth the bother
Save the Children/Save Us (repeat and fade)

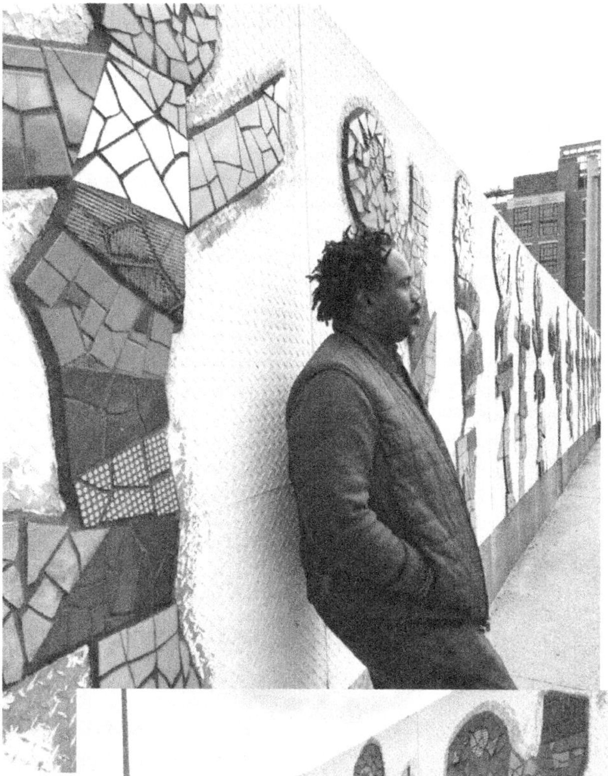

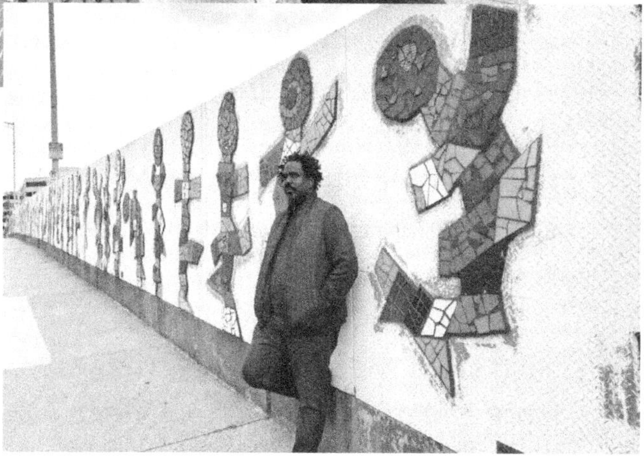

God is Love

To write this piece I have to take a moment and go to the multi disk CD package that I keep right behind me in my workspace. I opened it to read the words that Marvin Gaye wrote that were printed on the inside cover of the CD. I wanted to get this piece right, so I wanted to pull on more inspiration than the song. I remembered that Marvin spoke about God. Marvin wrote the following at the end of his statement:

"Find God: we've got to find the Lord. Allow him to influence us. I mean what other weapons have we to fight the forces

of hatred and evil. And check out the Ten Commandments too. You can't go too far wrong if you live them, dig it. Just a sincere and personal contact with God will keep you more together. Love the Lord, be thankful, feel peace. Thanks for life and loved ones. Thank you Jesus."

If we think about the people and or the things that we love in life
They require a level of submission on our part in order to fully enjoy the love within the relationship
This submission is done willfully and the difficulties within the process have a way of making our love grow stronger because we see ourselves as better "because of" than we would be "outside of"

The love(s) that we have in our lives have a way of shaping how we see ourselves and the world around us
In our love(s) we find our reasons for living and a sense of purpose in a

world that can make us feel worthless
Over time many have made the mistake of thinking that love is something that they get to define solely by the emotions and understandings of their mind
The combination of dual dysfunction leads to the appearance of function
The illusion of function alters the accuracy of the equation leaving you without the knowledge necessary to check your math, or evaluate or navigate your path

To understand the title of the track we have to have faith to see the scriptures as facts
John 3:16 explains the love that God had for the world which caused Him to send His Son.

The source of the forces of hatred and evil expressed throughout the

album with Marvin's pen, is identified by Jesus in John 10:10
"The thief does not come except to steal, and to kill, and to destroy. I have come that they may have life, and they may have it more abundantly."

Now if we dive into the song we recognize that God's love is strong
God's love has the power to forgive us of our sins
Take what the world has broken and make whole again
Give us a barometer to evaluate our friends
Provide the perspective to see our family as God sees us as His own

The song is a persuasion for us to love God because He first loved us
If we learn to love God then it's in God that we place our trust

Read the word to understand God's love has a plan for us
The transition of being a Father to becoming a Friend
Is one that happens over time through the transformation of heart, soul and mind

Marvin tells us to check out the 10 commandments, but Jesus came and captured all 10 in just two and He explains what they are Matthew chapter 22
"37 Jesus said to him, "*You shall love the Lord your God with all your heart, with all your soul, and with all your mind. 38 This is the first and great commandment. 39 And the second is like it, You shall love your neighbor as yourself. 40 On these two commandments hang all the Law and the Prophets.*"

God is love but how do I know what
that really means
If I don't take the time to study
1 Corinthians chapter 13
To compare it to love as defined in
1 John chapter 2
To know the difference between
God's love and love from the thief's
point of view

The scriptures tell us to not love in
word or in tongue, but in deed
and in truth
I can conjure up logic from math to
present a proof
If God is love then by the
commutative property love is God
But we live in a world that is
constantly changing making what's
simple seem so hard

God thank you for being love and
directing Yourself towards me

Giving me your spiritual eyes so the
truth in disguise which
are truthfully lies
Become clear to my natural eyes
and I press towards the prize

Jesus thank you for being my friend
at times when I felt alone
And loving me enough to reside in
my heart as a home
Now I can love the way You
desired us to all along
To bring life to the words
inside of Marvin's song
God is love God is love God is love
(fading out)

MERCY MERCY ME (The Ecology)

I turned on the tube and heard "Is this a natural disaster or a disaster being done to nature?"
Political views in competition with scientific news of climate change
A shift of a degree or two in my life span that would once represent a century or two
What must happen for us to listen to the cries of the earth?
The bloom from the seed of greed is blossoming at the expense of the signs of life

How close is the earth to a hearse where water is now a source of commerce?
The trauma of stolen land must be transferable in our DNA
Because generation after generation the people continue to act the same way

Breezes blocked by buildings as the Sun is dimmed by smog
Grass covered by cement streams redirected for power and pleasure
Projects designed like prisons and prisons designed like projects
So the differences between a tenant and an inmate isn't too great
The produce is produced to remain fresh only 'til you get it home
While what's on the corner calls the coroner with our expiration date
I have a stress disorder because things are out of order

But yet the medicine is only prescribed to me
And rest assured those pills ain't free
Can it be that I wasn't designed to live like this
And my disorder is my defense mechanism to trigger a fight in me to live
Live to challenge our thoughts of what has become the status quo

With all the differences we create between us to dispel the notion that there is an us
You would think that we've forgotten that we only have one planet to live on
We can dig to lay ourselves down or to plant a seed that will nourish our body and soul
With all the advancements and the inventions the earth still rotates and operates in seasons
Each has a purpose and are part of a larger plan

We claim to be so smart yet moving too fast to stop to understand
All that we need has already been provided
We don't have to create what has been God given
We just have to change our way of living
Stop valuing taking over giving
What we do today creates a tab that our children will have to pay tomorrow
And for many of our actions the debt will be paid in the currency of sorrow

Mercy Mercy Me let me study the sun, stream and tree
To understand the way that life is supposed to be
Mercy Mercy Me we live for the taking but what we devour isn't free
Help us understand that this isn't the way that life is supposed to be

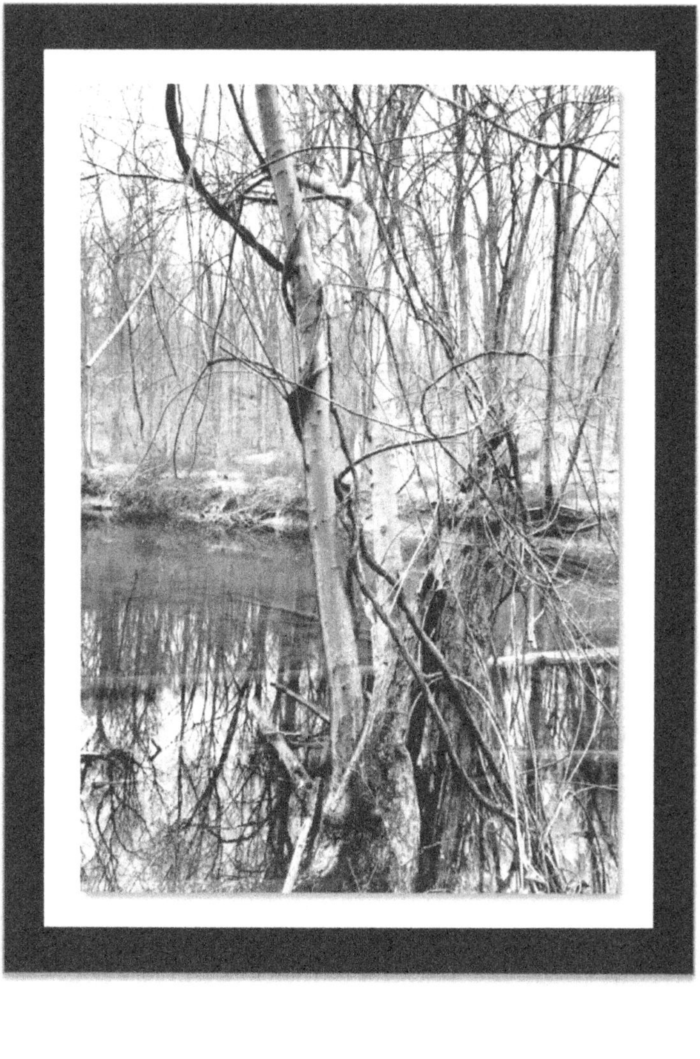

Right On

To the upbeat tempo I envision walking down the street to the spot where the brothers hang out
The cypher has started but I know how to enter on beat with a hand slap that sounds like a clap
This moment is special because it feels like all the brothers have come back to the hood
I see the pain of struggle on some faces while on others the smile of things being good
As words begin to fly and brothers turn to ministers, poets and philosophers
I see shorty taking mental notes because he realizes he's in the presence of life scholars

We all running this race called life, but the starting line isn't actually straight
This is a fact but to some they will debate along fault lines regardless of the system's design
Try running where you have to pay attention to the condition of the ground
A ground that is cracked, uneven, with shattered glass of broken dreams and faded blood from murder scenes.
This ground has absorbed the sounds of momma's screams
The children try to cover the sound by drawing with chalk along the path that they walk
A path that brings a smile while they hop past some on the bench drinking scotch

Some have figured a way out this craze, solved the maze with no remembrance of "yester-daze"

Is your responsibility because you have the ability to respond or because you know you owe
The scene that has been deemed destruction is also the blueprint of your construction
Take the world by storm because you've endured the seasons where tears and rain fell for different reasons
Both watered the ground and both caused seeds to bloom
One a source of energy and one a source of memory
Which one... the truth is they can interchange and almost become one in the same

Jay asked "How can I help the poor if I'm one of them/ So I got rich and gave back to me that's the win win"
A moment of clarity where wealth is only measured in the material attained by an individual

Poverty is such a cycle we can spend our
lives trying to find the point of origin
Is it systematic disguised as democratic
fooling us with lies disguised as a prize
telling us that we all can have it?
The it ... is the wealth that will cause us
not to be poor where 10 start the race but
there is only wealth for 4
Then the other 6 get told that they're
broken and themselves they have to fix
If one day, they want to become rich
And to the 4 they are told that they
should desire more
Sharing is a caring a song for children
not community building

Created skylines designed by redlines
concentrating crimes reappraising your
land in dollars while our currency is
dimes
Is this way that world was designed to go
round on its axis

How does it feel being back on the block where you once stood
In your fine apparel telling everyone that life is good
You give a few hugs and a few pounds knowing that when the street lights come on you're nowhere to be found
We can start by rebuilding the park
And this time let's place art on the heart creating murals that live and breathe
Children as priceless works with a purpose to achieve
Zip codes expanding our territory instead of dividing our lanes
Seeing each other as God sees us where we're one in the same

Those who have and those who have not both have a value inside that is needed to be given
This is the secret that is revealed when love is used as the force for our living

Not the love of wealth or even the love of self but the love of health
Health that is contingent of the condition of the community
Where we understand what we have in common and the power of our unity

Now what I do may not be for you to do because God is ordering my steps
But you do have something to do if you just take a look around
See what speaks to your soul and where your joy is found
For some it's at the school where the children congregate, and teachers educate
For some it's at the center where the seniors dwell with stories to tell
For some it's at the church where they're saying that Jesus is coming soon
For some it's at the job center where people are trying to reenter from being a prisoner

For some it's the college where you have the opportunity to share your knowledge
For some it's in the park where the brothers playing chess to plot, plan and relieve stress
For some it's on the corner where moments create makeshift memorials of the lost

Wherever it is find your love and your place to give
There really is no greater way to live
When I say right on I mean keep going, keep showing and keep growing
When I say right on I mean stay right there because you're making an impact and the people know that you care
When I say right on I mean that you are on the front line in your right mind loving according to God's design
When I say right on I stand with a clenched fist with veins showing in my wrist

Not ready to punch but to show how hard
I'm holding on
To the things that make us strong... Right on
To the things that make us strong... Right on
To the things that make us strong... Right on

Wholy Holy

John 1:1 In the beginning was the Word and the Word was with God and the Word was God.

Proverbs 12:1 Whoever loves instruction loves knowledge, But he who hates correction is stupid.

Everyone is invited but I know everyone won t like it and everyone won t recite it
An attack will come because this love talk will be perceived as exclusionary
Because I m speaking for a moment about the destruction of the adversary

A warfare that is spiritual has become a battle where the combatants are individual

Im writing this piece in the midst of an overcast of clouds full of doubt death and despair while looking for a ray of hope in the glimmer of sunshine. Understanding that on the cloudiest days the sun is present even when it is unseen. I get through these days based on the knowledge of the truth. If we live our lives where our physical eyes must see the proof then we are living a life that is absent of faith.

I can find reasons in the midst of any season to practically justify my sin based on how I feel within. I am a victim who has decided that it is time to administer pain. They look at me like there is a beast within that makes

me different from them so from this point
let the reign of the wolves begin. No more
disguised like a sheep I m going to become
comfortable being the beast. Societal chains
constrict more than physical ones because
when I say that I am chained by society few
people believe me. So much so that I can
begin to doubt myself. Is this an excuse to
not produce or is this a truth that I have
been dealing with from my youth?

In the midst of this crazy scene I m led to
read Hebrews 12:14; "Pursue peace with all
people and holiness without which no one
will see the Lord." Lord I need to do more
than see you I need to feel you and be with
you. Not only when this phase of life is
over I need to know that you ve got my back
when I check over my shoulder. Better yet I

need you to take the lead because I don't know how to proceed. How do I pursue peace with those who see me as less than human? How do I pursue peace with those who have historically and to this day are the beneficiaries of my tears my blood my strength and my mind? How do I pursue peace with those who don't believe that You exist? How do I pursue peace within myself when the presence of evil always persists?

At times I close my eyes to not cry but yet the tears still seep out and swim down my cheeks to land into my palms. Nightmares robbing sleep to the point that I have to wake up to feel calm. Living in reverse is like calling Your blessings a curse because before I can see a change in others You're requiring a change in me first. Lord I was born this way its in my DNA and You re telling me that all of this can change if I have enough faith to pray I want to I really do but at times I don t know what to say.

What does it mean to be wholy holy ? I know the song and I do my best to sing along to feel strong so that I can press on. In the song it says that Jesus You will return and in Your Word there is so much for us to learn. If class is in session then where do I start... Hebrews 4:12 "For the word of God *is* living and powerful and sharper than any two edged sword piercing even to the division of soul and spirit and of joints and marrow and is a discerner of the thoughts and intents of the heart."

So holiness begins with me looking in the mirror regardless of what is out my window. You've empowered me with the strength to not allow what may happen to me to control me. With your eyes I can see people in a way that will lead me to pray instead of seeing them as prey and a defense to me feeling hunted. Jesus it's you that has been and will be the keeper of my soul. Jesus it's you that has been the holder of the piece which is Your peace that I need to feel whole.

I'm reminded of a line from an L Boogie song that says "The chain of satan wasn't made that strong." I see that if I learn to resist the chains will be gone.

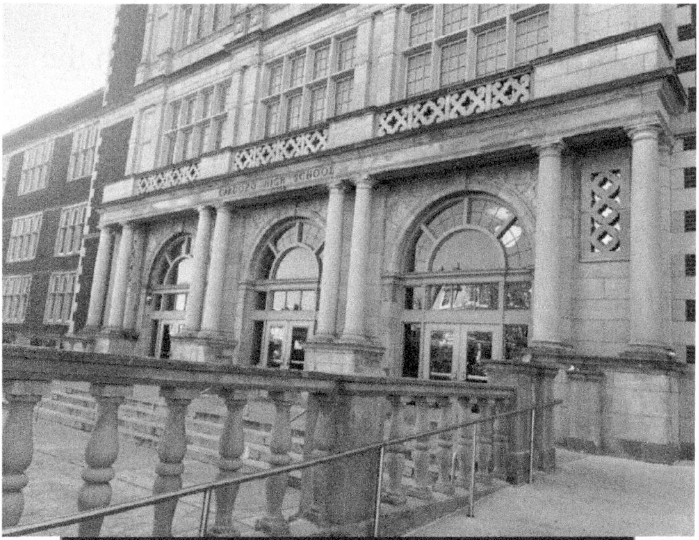

INNER CITY BLUES
(Makes Me Wanna Holler)

My people have been hollering so loud and for so long I see the words in the air

The breeze in my town has the sound of faint cries for justice and freedom

The breath used to raise my voice may need to be used to hold on to life

Marvin told us about trigger happy policing and crime increasing

So may be my hollering is the way of my trauma and toxins releasing

The air that carries this virus of sorrow and pain seems to be incurable strain

Shot by a bullet instead of a vaccine ... eyes closed to meet death instead of to dream

Resources allotted by greed instead of allotted by need

Education as a way out instead of learning how to make a change

But the inner city has a rhythm of its own that is produced by those who call it home

My EQ contains highs, mids and lows that adjust at times so the flow is exposed

Remember it is out of the concrete here that rose grows

Watered with the mixture of rain, tears and memory pours

Raising up from the ground ready for whatever life has in store

Navigation of a system that we protest is broken

When the truth is... it is operating according to its design

Without you and me in mind at the same time its designers made sure they were fine

Overtaxed with under representation and this is presented as freedom

From our ancestor's existence in forced occupation without compensation

Can I holler for them? Growing up to be disrespected as women and men

Trying their hardest to stay afloat while fantasizing about getting ahead

Heart skipping in beat with the siren sounds hoping no one is dead

Living in the inner city is living at best on borrowed ground

Because we've seen what happens when the yuppies decide to come in town

The children of those who grew up with a yard and fence

Decide to trade their space for place with an elevator and elevated rents

The dollars to be earned tomorrow to them are on sale today for cents

Red lines on my test paper and around my neighborhood

Denied entry because I was told that neither my school or credit are good

The Blues are about looking at today full of its gloom

While still finding a way to make a tune

The melodies of moans serve as a chorus for hope being sung

You know up the road today a man was hung

You can still hear momma humming "we shall overcome"

I know some prefer "we gon' be alright" because they're ready to fight

Fists balled tight and raised straight in the air punching at the clouds

Children of the children of the generation that was told to say it loud

In 2021 how do we show that we're black and proud

I love my skin that gets cast in the shadow of sin before my time even begins

Where mere survival in the inner city is classified as a win

But it's no longer enough to just be a pawn in the game

It's time to commit my mind to board, piece and rule design

They emphasize thinking as the difference between checkers and chess

Where the moves you make today impacts the moves you will make tomorrow

But the moves that I'm making today are my own or am I being controlled

Thinking I'm free with my body but what about my mind and soul?

The blues are an iteration of gospel's hope

It's therapeutic the way we do it when the cypher laments

The inner city forced us together to make it all make sense

The inner city found a way to teach us love and pride

Not with a price tag on a rack but what you have inside

We have a way to shine everyday regardless of the weather

With expanded definitions of family that keeps us together

I realize that Marvin's first and last song lyric between What's Going On and Inner City Blues was to the Mothers

There is something special about the mothers that find faith in the midst of mourning

A mother's love is a manifestation of life itself even when it's rejected by her children

She has a way to be there for everyone else often at the sacrifice of herself

Let us begin to live on behalf of the mothers

Let our choices begin to dry their tears and alleviate her fears

The sight of a mother is our eyes being open to see that God is real

The inner city mothers have a way of seeing all the children on the block as their own

The love of our mothers should make us brothers and sisters

Making the landscape of the inner city the portrait of one family picture

The love of our mothers should make us brothers and sisters

Making the landscape of the inner city the portrait of one family picture

WHERE ARE WE GOING?

Day In ... Day Out
What's going on?
What's it all about?
Where are we going?
What is life showing?
Day In ... Day Out

I'm inspired
When people truly get tired
When "enough is enough" goes from a
solo to a choir
Then I know that we are ready to go higher
It's not enough to get tired of what we see
We have to have the vision to see a
different destiny
We must see ourselves loving one another

In a way that makes us sisters and
brothers
What makes us different and keeps
us apart
Is the aspiration of the evil one's heart
We've been tricked to believe that
different has to result in one being better
If I'm always being viewed as inferior what
is my motivation to ever get together

What will it take for us to acknowledge the
level of hate
That it takes to determine a child's fate by
their birthplace
When equity is pictured as giving a child a
view from behind the fence
And judges must be English teachers the
way they construct a sentence
Race records reclassified as Rhythm
and Blues
Does this mean that I can EQ my suffering
for your listening enjoyment

Or master the sound that was made when master wasn't around
A song can reveal a state of confusion and spark a revolution
Words that are heard contain a power surge that can lift hearts and strike nerves
Words in rhyme can ignite minds to create blueprint designs
To architect the times with our future in the lines
The lessons captured in the dimensions and the depth of the illustration
Where are we headed as a generation, a nation and a civilization

Educate to assimilate or to elevate
Educate to recreate or to create
Educate to cooperate or to advocate
Educate to annihilate or to liberate
Day In ... Day Out
What's going on?
What's it all about?

Where are we going?
What is life showing?
Day In ... Day Out

Skepticism grows
As some in the church are exposed
I got vaccinated
But to some I'm still hated
Before my ID is checked
I'm treated as a threat
The position of death is six feet deep
Or six cramped in a space with no room to sleep
Or six memorials for young people on one street
Or six users intaking... (the bridge) where "giving up" and "giving in" meet
Six times four is twenty-four
A day in the life
Of those who wished for more
What will you do with your six times four

That will show where are we going ... for
our next six times four
What will you do with your six times four
That will show where are we going ... for
our next six times four

Day In ... Day Out
What's going on?
What's it all about?
Where are we going?
What is life showing?
Day In ... Day Out

Made in the USA
Middletown, DE
21 July 2023